THIS WAY TO LIFE

DISCOVERING LIFE TO THE FULL

Derek Prime

This Way to Life: Discovering life to the full
Copyright © 2011 Derek Prime (Reprinted 2013, 2016)

Fully revised edition. A previous edition
of this book was published in 1968.

Published by 10Publishing, a division of 10ofthose.com
Ten Of Those Ltd, Unit C
Tomlinson Road Leyland PR25 2DY
Email: info@10ofthose.com
Website: www.10ofthose.com

British Library Cataloguing in Publication Data. A catalogue
record for this book is available from the British Library

ISBN: 9781906173159

Cover design by Diane Bainbridge
Printed by CPI Group (UK) Ltd, Croydon, England, CR0 4YY

CONTENTS

Give the Facts

Imagine we are in the middle of an election campaign. Each candidate wants to win our vote. As we listen to them, we are aware that they have carefully rehearsed what they are going to say in answer to hard questions and that there is a degree of spin or manipulative tactics behind their answers.

We may feel the same when a variety of views are presented to us by the religions of the world. We believe the truth is out there somewhere – but where? What we long for is the honest truth – the presentation of the unvarnished facts. 'Simply tell us the truth!' is what we long to say.

Facts do speak for themselves. The purpose of this book is to provide the facts about Christianity. Its title, *This Way to Life*, is a true description of Christianity because Jesus Christ said to His disciples, 'I am the way and the truth and the life' (John 14:6). They proved His words to be true and so have millions upon millions of others.

The words we have just quoted are from the Bible because that is where we find the truth, the facts about Christianity and Jesus Christ who is at its centre. Therefore, without apology, many quotations from the Bible will be given, as well as where in the Bible back up can be found for statements that are made.

We probably begin our search for the truth because of challenges we face in life. Life is far from exciting and fulfilling for many of us. Worries, troubles and problems may weigh us down, particularly if we are middle-aged or older; while living for 'kicks' – perhaps because of the fear of boredom – marks some who are younger. What's life all about anyway? Has it any purpose? Can it be satisfying? Some are afraid of asking such questions, sensing that their disillusionment may increase if they fail to find any answers.

And then what about the end of life, that is to say, death? Is it really the end? Something deep down in the majority, if not all of us, suggests that death cannot be the termination of our existence. There is a hereafter, although what it is, we do not know.

'This way to life,' Christianity shouts out to a world that is too noisy for the most part to listen. Through Jesus Christ life in the here and now can be what God originally intended it to be – the experience of knowing God personally as our friend and helper, with the purpose and fulfillment such a relationship with Him brings.

'This way to life,' Christianity proclaims confidently at the grave or the crematorium, breaking into the blackness of dress and the dismalness of conversation, like the sun breaking through a sky dark with ominous clouds.

Part of our problem is that having hundreds of slogans flung at us every day from hoardings, newspapers, magazines, and television commercials, we easily pass off anything new that is presented as belonging to the general run of things – lots of empty talk without much of value in it.

But pause a moment. The issues – when it comes to Christianity – are too great to parcel up with the passing slogans and issues we see or hear every day. 'This way to life' is not an advertising slogan but an accurate description of Christianity. At rock bottom, Christianity, as said earlier, is all about the Lord Jesus Christ, who said, '*I am the way, the truth and the life*' (John 14:6). How then can we know that Christianity is the right way? And if it is, how do we find it? And what do we do when we have? To provide the answers that the Bible gives to these questions is the purpose of this book. So let us start at the beginning.

1 God has spoken

The silence – if ever there was one – has been broken. God does have something to say to us. He wants to communicate with men and women, whom He has made. He is not the indifferent Creator some of His creatures would like to suggest He is.

Think, for a moment, what the position would be like if God had not spoken. Thoughts we have about God would be beyond confirmation. Certainty about His existence and character would be impossible. Any discussion of the purpose of human life would be mere speculation.

But God *has* spoken. He has *not* left His creation in ignorance. Opinions about Him can be tested.

God has used, and still uses, three main approaches through which to speak to us – one is indirect, and the others direct and pointed.

1. God's creation

We sometimes say that 'Actions speak louder than words.' If we come home from work and find a meal both ready and carefully prepared for us, the meal itself shows that someone is concerned for our well-being. So it is with the world God has made: it overflows with actions which reveal God's character. But just as children sometimes take for granted their mother's love and care, and even fail to notice them, so also we sometimes live with our eyes 'shut' to what God's creation says to us. Nevertheless, the evidence is there.

God's creation shows that He exists. The created world displays many strong evidences of thought. Take, for example, the human body, which doctors, surgeons, and ordinary people all recognise as a most wonderful piece of machinery. The inevitable conclusion, therefore, is that where there is thought, there must be a Thinker (Genesis 1:3, 31; Isaiah 55:5, 9).

Laws are found in the creation. The sun and the earth, for instance, follow clearly definable laws (Psalm 19:4-6). Is it not reasonable to conclude, therefore, that where there are laws, there must be a Law-Giver?

The created world teems with life (Genesis 7:15; 26:12-14). Programmes on television take us to the farthest parts of the world, and reveal the immense variety of life there is on this planet. But where there is life, there must be a Life-Giver (Acts 17:25).

Creation shouts out to us that God exists. 'The heavens declare the glory of God; the skies proclaim the work of his hands' (Psalm 19:1). And it proclaims most clearly His kindness.

My wife and I rented a small country cottage for a week's holiday. Arranging it all by correspondence, and the owners not being there to greet us, we did not meet them. But we had not stayed long in their cottage – so very much their 'creation' – without learning much about them. Taste in decorations, concern for neatness and cleanliness and love of colour; things like these spoke out although the owners were not there.

His love to us is seen in the everyday things of human life which we take so often for granted...

If we look 'with our eyes open', at what God has made, it clearly speaks of Him. His love to us is seen in the everyday things of human life which we take so often for granted, such as food, water, the elements, the seasons, the 'balance of nature' and its resources. God generously gives us all these things for our enjoyment and profit.

On an island in the middle of the Irish Sea, the actress Julie Andrews 'witnessed the total solar eclipse that travelled over Europe. Never a visibly religious woman, she admitted sensing "forces, way, way out there mysteriously keeping the world in a kind of balance."' She thought, 'there must be a God' (Richard Stirling: *Julie Andrews: An Intimate Biography, p5*)

2. The Bible

God's second line of approach is the Bible. The word *Bible* comes from a Greek word meaning *books*. It is a suitable title because it contains sixty-six books. If we think of someone's home or a children's school classroom in which there are two bookshelves, we have a picture of the Bible. The top shelf – what we call *The Old Testament (39 books)* - is there to prepare the way by its promises for the coming of Jesus into the world – and the bottom shelf, *The New Testament (27 books)*, tells us that what was promised happened more than two thousand years ago and is relevant to us today.

The Bible is a unique communication from God to us (2 Timothy 3:16). Unashamedly, the Bible claims that God is its source – it claims to be 'inspired' or 'breathed' by Him'. More than 500 times in the first five books of the Bible alone, God's authority is claimed for what is written (e.g. Deuteronomy 4:5; Exodus 20:1). The New Testament says that the Old Testament is inspired (1 Peter 1:10ff; 2 Peter 1:21; 2 Timothy 3:16), and quotes it as final authority.

The Lord Jesus Christ promised inspiration to His apostles (John 14:26; 15:26-27; 16:13), and, not surprisingly, therefore, they claimed to possess it (Acts 2:33; 15:28; 1 Thessalonians 1:5; 4:8; 1 Corinthians 4:1). And from their inspired writings arose what we know as the New Testament.

Understandably, some will say, 'But how do we know that the Bible is inspired?' If by 'know' we mean 'have scientific proof', the answer is that it cannot be established. But there are all kinds of evidence which indicate that the Bible is inspired.

Let's begin with the Bible's age. Age, in and of itself, proves nothing, but we cannot overlook the Bible's age in that it has stood the test of time. We can explain the fact that although it has so often been attacked, it has still been preserved, only if we accept that God has intervened on its behalf.

The Bible is made up of sixty-six different books, written by more than forty authors, over a great stretch of human history, yet it has perfect unity and harmony throughout. This points dramatically to its inspiration by God; and so does the fact that its prophecies have been fulfilled (Deuteronomy 28:64; cf. Jeremiah 30:11; Micah 5:2; Zechariah 9:9; 11:12-13).

Knowledge of human nature, remarkable frankness and honesty when dealing with its heroes, together with superb moral teaching all serve to lift the Bible on to a plane unparalleled by all other writings. The Lord Jesus Christ in His teaching often referred to the Old Testament as the Word of God (Mark 12:36; Matthew 5:18), adding confirmation to the fact that the Bible has God directly as its source.

But the most important 'proof' for Christians of the Bible's inspiration is the fact that they find God actually speaking to them personally through it: so clearly that their lives are changed through it. The Bible is God's voice. When the Bible speaks, God speaks.

Every Christmas I hear from a friend of my student days. We often talked about the Christian faith but he remained sceptical. When the time came for the long summer holidays I suggested to him that he read John's Gospel through and that, if he felt able, to pray for God's help to know whether what he read was true or not. Half way through the vacation, he wrote, 'You'll probably be surprised to hear that at last I have made my peace with God and am discovering all that I have been missing.'

Not enough

The voice of God through the Bible, however, was not enough.

The spiritual deafness of the human race means that the words of God are not heard. We all begin life far away and out of touch with God. An American newsreader captured his hearers' attention as he told a meaningful story on Christmas day. A husband decided to have done with his annual farce of insincere church-attendance on the Sunday evening before Christmas Day. His wife might go alone; he would remain at home. She left the house to go to the church service. Snow fell heavily. The curtains were open, the lights were on, and the husband felt self-satisfied at the strength of his convictions. Suddenly, there were bumps on the window. Birds had hit the glass, attracted by the bright light of the room, shining out in the darkness. Having hit the window with force, they laid half-stunned by the impact. The husband's instinct was to help them, concerned at their bewilderment. Quickly he conceived a plan. He opened the doors of the barn where they could find shelter for the night from the snow. To attract them, he put on the lights in the barn. But it was useless; they made no move to the barn. He tried to catch them one by one without success. Frustrated, he watched them, and exclaimed, 'You foolish, stubborn creatures! I want to help you, but you won't let me. I guess I would have to become a bird – to be just like you – to be able to get through to you and help.' And at that precise moment the church bells rang – the Christmas bells – and he remembered. He suddenly understood why God Himself became a human being, like us, in the person of Jesus Christ.

> **God could not have spoken more convincingly and powerfully than He has in His Son.**

3. Jesus Christ

'In the past God spoke to our forefathers through the prophets at many times and in various ways, but in these last days he has spoken to us by His Son, whom he appointed heir of all things, and through whom he made the universe' (Hebrews 1:1-2). This is the great truth the Bible unfolds: God has spoken to us through His Son, Jesus Christ. We are the visited planet.

The Lord Jesus Christ is the visible image of the invisible God (Colossians 1:15-17). No one has ever seen God at any time, but Jesus has made Him known. Jesus Himself said, 'Anyone who has seen me has seen the Father' (John 14:9). As He lived among the men and women of the first century, they witnessed His majesty and glory, such as only belongs to God (John 1:14). The human Jesus, who could be looked at, watched and touched, was seen to be the Son of God (1 John 1:1-3). All miracles bore witness to the truth that He is God (John 20:30, 31): most of all, the miracle of His resurrection (Romans 1:1-4). The more Jesus' claims are tested, the more convincing they become.

God could not have spoken more convincingly and powerfully than He has in His Son. His love for the world stands out as we understand that He was willing to send His only Son into the world (John 3:16). To hear Jesus Christ is to hear God. To read His words is to read God's words.

God has spoken: creation, the Bible, and Jesus Himself stand before us for investigation. To be ignorant about God is unnecessary – and cannot be excused. If we question sincerely, we shall find an answer – that God has spoken; and we need to listen to what He says.

2 | God cares

'I can't believe that God is interested in little me,' said an elderly man who seemed desperately to want to believe in God. In speaking like this, he was failing to realise the meaning of the fact that God *has* spoken. Speaking shows that someone cares. A wife whose husband is perpetually silent might say with justice, 'He doesn't really care, for he never speaks to me.'

But God has spoken; and that speaking demonstrates His care for us. The creation through which God continually speaks indicates His concern for us. Everything about creation is geared to the good of men and women. God 'causes His sun to rise on the evil and the good, and sends rain on the righteous and the unrighteous' (Matthew 5:45); 'he is kind to the ungrateful and wicked' (Luke 6:35).

The Bible, through which God speaks, tells us about His interest in our well-being. 'His compassions never fail. They are new every morning; great is your faithfulness' (Lamentations 3:22, 23). God takes thought for the poor and needy and delivers them (Psalm 40:17). The every-day burdens of life may be cast upon Him (1 Peter 5:7).

The laws of the Bible reveal God's care and concern for all His creatures. Admittedly they also reflect God's own character and His hatred of wrong-doing too. But they display His desire for our true well-being. God's laws put a rightful restraint upon our behaviour. Imagine a society with people encouraged to dishonour their parents, killing as they wish, committing adultery without check, stealing as suits them, lying and being jealous of what others have. The thought is horrifying.

The Lord Jesus Christ said a lot about God's care. He took up what is small and insignificant to illustrate it. 'Are not five sparrows sold for two pennies? Yet not one of them is forgotten by God. Indeed, the very hairs of your head are all numbered. Don't be afraid; you are worth more than many sparrows' (Luke 12:6-7). 'Look at the birds of the air; they do not sow or reap or store away in barns, and yet your heavenly Father feeds them. Are you not much more valuable than they? Who of you by worrying can add a single hour to his life? And why do you worry about clothes? See how the lilies of the field grow. They do not labour or spin. Yet I tell you that not even Solomon in all his splendour was dressed like one of these. If that is how God clothes the grass of the field, which is here today and tomorrow is thrown into the fire, will he not much more clothe you, O you of little faith'? (Matthew 6:26-30). Our physical well-being, our food, our life span, our clothing are all declared to be ways in which God cares for us.

Jesus demonstrated God's care in the things He said and did. He healed the blind and the suffering: He never ignored anyone who needed Him. He cared for society's 'untouchables', like the leper – touching and healing him! He comforted the bereaved. He gave Himself most of all to those who were spoken of in a critical way as 'sinners'. He sought out the outcast with love. As the visible image of the invisible God, He displayed God's care.

Above all, the Lord Jesus Christ proved God's care and concern for us in His death on the cross (Titus 3:4). When He came into the world to die as the Saviour for sinners, He revealed beyond question the supreme goodness and unspeakable kindness of God. The Cross was a horrible experience for Him to suffer, and equally dreadful for His Father to permit. But God loved the world so much that He gave His only Son to die for sinners in this way.

Care and love

Care springs from love: 'God is love' (1 John 4:8). Of necessity, in His very nature, and for ever, God is love. Everything about Him sets forth His love. All His ways are loving and faithful (Psalm 25:10). 'This is how God showed his love among us: he sent his one and only Son into the world that we might live through him. This is love: not that we loved God, but that he loved us and sent his Son as an atoning sacrifice for our sins' (1 John 4:9-10). When we are perplexed by the world's suffering, which we cannot easily equate with a God who cares, if we then look at the Cross, we will realize that God has a purpose in the suffering He permits in this world.

God's greatness – 'little me'

'I can't believe that God is interested in "little me"', the man said. God's greatness is actually seen and demonstrated in His care for us as individuals. Our idea of greatness is coloured by our experience as human beings. When a person becomes great or important - or perhaps a celebrity - we begin to feel, 'Well, he or she can't have time for me any more.' But Jesus taught that human ideas about greatness have to be reversed because they are so often out of keeping with God's character (Mark 10:37-45). The almighty and everlasting God cares for every individual. No one else could either contemplate or achieve such a feat. His care is so personal and perfect that it is in marked contrast to the care men and women have for one another, even at its best.

God cares! Consider His love in creation. Think about the statements of the Bible. See the care Jesus showed – God the Father's care. View the Cross. We may feel we do not deserve such care, and think, 'But why? Who are we to be the recipients of such love?' But God loves men and women so much that He is not concerned whether or not we deserve His love (Ephesians 2:9; Titus 3:4-5); rather His concern is that we should understand and respond to His love as He has revealed it in the gift of His Son and

His Son's death in the place of sinners, taking the righteous anger sin deserves.

God's love and care rightly move us when we really appreciate them. William Temple, an Archbishop of Canterbury, wrote of his father, 'My father, who was described by one who knew him as "granite on fire" and was certainly never regarded as sentimental, could not speak of the love of God without tears.' God's kindness is meant to lead us to repentance, that is, to turn us from our wrong-doing, back to God, determined to obey Him (Romans 2:4).

3 Separated from God

When a husband and wife sadly 'separate', behind the break-down of the relationship there often lies a history of quarrels and disagreements. If children are involved, they inevitably suffer from the action of their parents. The barrier which separates their parents works its way into the children's lives.

Barriers mean separation. For more than twenty-eight years East Germany was cut off from West Germany by the Berlin wall; and the existence and sight of that wall was a reminder and illustration of the barrier that exists between God and us.

The sad truth we need to understand is that our sins separate us from God. 'Your iniquities [persistently doing wrong] have separated you from your God; your sins have hidden his face from you, so that he will not hear,' declares the prophet Isaiah (Isaiah 59:2). The fact that many people even deny God's very existence shows how much men and women are separated from God. Others, however, do not deny God's existence but live without any thought of Him. They could not care less about how God says they should live. As James says, 'Now listen, you who say, "Today or tomorrow we will go to this or that city, spend a year there, carry on business and make money." Why, you do not even know what will happen tomorrow. What is your life? You are a mist that appears for a little while and then vanishes. Instead, you ought to say, "If it is the Lord's will, we will live and do this or that." As it is, you boast and brag. All such boasting is evil' (James 4:13-16). In other words, 'We can manage our own affairs: thank you very much,' we say, or imply by our attitude.

The separation proves real enough for many of us when we try to pray: our prayers seem to achieve nothing. They are no part of a fixed or established friendship with God, as they could be.

The cause

There is no beating about the bush in the Bible: the cause of separation is sin. 'Your iniquities have separated you from your God; your sins have hidden his face from you, so that he will not hear' (Isaiah 59:2). We can see that this is true if we put ourselves up against the Ten Commandments (Exodus 20:3-17). They are rather like a plumb-line or straight-edge. God's law is the standard by which all of our lives must be tested. Here they are:

First 'You shall have no other gods before me' (Exodus 20:3). God requires first place in our affections. He is to be our true Master. He alone deserves our worship. Whenever we give something or some person other than God first place in our affections – as, for example, friendships, ambitions, possessions – we break this first law.

Second 'You shall not make for yourself an idol in the form of anything in heaven above or on the earth beneath or in the waters below. You shall not bow down to them or worship them' (Exodus 20:4, 5). Idols and images of God are forbidden. Idols are not only objects made of wood or stone but people, ambitions and possessions that occupy the place in our lives that God alone should have. Our society has idols in the world of entertainment and sport. We may foolishly have greater regard or respect for them than God. But the commandment does not end there. It also means that if we go through the form of worshipping God, but forget that God is Spirit, and so do not worship Him sincerely from our hearts, we are breaking this commandment.

> **Idols are not only objects made of wood or stone but people, ambitions and possessions**

Third 'You shall not misuse the name of the Lord your God, for the Lord will not hold anyone guiltless who misuses his name' Exodus 20:7). Loose language, including, of course, swearing and glib and insincere talk about God is condemned here.

Fourth 'Remember the Sabbath day by keeping it holy. Six days you shall labour and do all your work, but the seventh day is a Sabbath to the Lord your God. On it you shall not do any work, neither you, nor your son or daughter, nor your manservant or maidservant, nor your animals, nor the alien within your gates. For in six days the Lord made the heavens and the earth, the sea, and all that is in them, but he rested on the seventh day. Therefore the Lord blessed the Sabbath day and made it holy' (Exodus 20:8-11). One day in seven belongs to God, and so we are to use it for Him. This means we should not do unnecessary work ourselves, or cause others to work.

Fifth 'Honour your father and your mother, so that you may live long in the land the Lord your God is giving you' (Exodus 20:12). Sadly, the world of which we are part witnesses the break down of family life, not least through child abuse. But if our parents have honestly done their best for us in our upbringing they are to be respected, especially as they get older.

Sixth 'You shall not murder' (Exodus 20:13). We are to love our enemies and 'do good to those who hate us' (Luke 6:27). It is not only physical murder that is intended. We sometimes say, *'If looks could kill…'* The Lord Jesus Christ showed the full extent of the commandment when He said, 'You have heard that it was said to the people long ago, "Do not murder, and anyone who murders will be subject to judgment." But I tell you that anyone who is angry with his brother will be subject to judgment. Again, anyone who says to his brother, "Raca," is answerable to the Sanhedrin. But anyone who says, "You fool!" will be in danger of the fire of hell. ('Raca' was an Aramaic word - the language spoken in first century Palestine - and was an insult in that it declared someone to be empty-headed.) Therefore, if you are offering your gift at the altar and there remember that your brother has something against you, leave your gift there in front of the altar. First go and be reconciled to your brother; then come and offer your gift'(Matthew 5:21-24).

Seventh 'You shall not commit adultery' (Exodus 20:14). All forms of immorality are included. Our Lord's command shows this: 'You have heard that it was said, "Do not commit adultery." But I tell you that anyone who looks at a woman lustfully has already committed adultery with her in his heart' (Matthew 5:27-28). If we take pleasure in sexually provocative literature, web-sites, plays, films and the like, we break this commandment. Further, what we think about automatically influences what we do when we are tempted.

Eighth 'You shall not steal' (Exodus 20:15). Avoiding the right payment of income tax, dodging customs, taking our employer's possessions, leaving work before time, all these come under the axe of this commandment. Employers, too, should remember that this commandment means giving just wages and a square deal in business.

Ninth 'You shall not give false testimony against your neighbour' (Exodus 20:16). Talking about people unkindly, and listening to how other people criticize them, are included. Repeating a false story, gossipping and murmuring – all those ways in which we may misuse our tongues fall under its judgment. This commandment protects other people's reputations.

Tenth 'You shall not covet your neighbour's house. You shall not covet your neighbour's wife, or his manservant or maidservant, his ox or donkey, or anything that belongs to your neighbour' (Exodus 20:17) Coveting is wanting something we ought not to have, whether because it does not belong to us, or because we cannot really afford to buy it, or for other reasons. We can easily see that the number of things we can covet is countless; also that coveting lies at the root of many other sins, such as stealing and adultery.

All guilty

If we honestly try to keep these commandments, we soon realize that we are quite unable to do so. Some foolishly imagine that they can keep God's commandments; they think this because they have never taken them seriously, perhaps treating them rather like parking regulations – useful sometimes, but rather a bore, and to be avoided where possible. We may even deliberately oppose any thought of God's laws having a place in our life. I do not know who put it there but I remember seeing a sticker on the side of a post-box in Edinburgh that read: 'Please keep your laws out of my life.'

As we examine our failure to obey the Ten Commandments we see how great the barrier is between God and ourselves. The truth is that we inherited a sinful nature from our parents as they did from theirs – a process which has gone on since in the beginning humanity rebelled against God. Like a bowl in a game of bowls, we have a natural bias to evil. There is not a day in my life that I've lived as I know I ought, whether in my thoughts, words or actions. At birth we are full of the natural poison of sin (Mark 7:15, 20-3; Matthew 15:11, 15-20) – rather like a newly hatched snake. This unhappy predicament provides no excuse for our sins, but aggravates them. It is because we *are* sinners that we *do* sin.

We have offended God, flouted His authority, gone against Him, put ourselves in the wrong with Him – in fact, made ourselves His open enemies. 'There is not a righteous man on earth who does good and never sins' (Ecclesiastes 7:20). All miss the mark. Like our throwing pebbles at a tin can on the beach, we may be lucky to hit the target from time to time, but for the most part we fall short or go too far. 'All have turned away, they have together become worthless; there is no-one who does good, not even one' (Romans 3:12).

An inevitable barrier

God cannot look upon sinful men and women and be pleased with them. The relationship He intended to have with them has been completely spoilt and broken. He can have no fellowship with those who live in disobedience to His laws, for His laws spring from His holiness, and when we disobey, this is the very opposite of the holiness which pleases God.

Holiness is the first feature of God's character with which we are confronted in the Bible (Psalm 24:3; Isaiah 6:3). It is a way of expressing His moral perfection. He is majestic in holiness (Exodus 15:11); there is no one holy like Him (1 Samuel 2:2). His holiness is such that He cannot overlook wickedness and dishonesty (Micah 6:10-13); He is of purer eyes than to stand evil and cannot look on wrong (Habakkuk 1:13). The inevitable reaction of God against sin is wrath, or anger, for sin contradicts His perfection. Wrath is the recoil of His perfection against wrong.

If we see our sin only in comparison with other people's, we probably let ourselves off too easily. We see sin properly when we see it against the background of God's holiness.

But the effects of sin go beyond this life. If nothing is done about our separation from God in this life, we will be separated from God for ever. We are sorry when we part from those we love. But how dreadful will be the sorrow of those who part from God and His people for ever. Hell is the place where men and women are for ever separated from God. To be cast into hell is to be separated from the Lord Jesus Christ, to be cursed and to be eternally punished (Matthew 25:46). It means eternal exclusion from the radiance of the face of the Lord, and the glorious majesty of His power (2 Thessalonians 1:9).

Sin is our greatest problem, much as some may think otherwise. John Knox, a well-known sixteenth century Christian, wrote, 'In youth, middle age, and now after many battles, I find nothing in me but vanity and corruption.' If we have become aware of our sin, we may be encouraged, for God makes us realize how ill we are before He makes us better.

4 | We are of ourselves helpless

'Hell is before me.' Such a prospect is enough to make us try to save ourselves. And at first sight it may seem easy enough to achieve. After all, we overcome most difficulties: why not this one?

But we cannot help ourselves when it comes to the problem of our separation from God. God tells us this is so. 'Can the Ethiopian change his skin or the leopard its spots? Neither can you do good who are accustomed to doing evil' (Jeremiah 13:23). When it comes to sin, we are far from having things under control. Lust, theft, murder, adultery, greed, wickedness, deceit, sensuality, envy, slander, arrogance and folly plague human life, and individual human lives.

Helplessness

We cannot remove the record of the past. Many of our past sins may still dog our footsteps. God, the Judge, completely knows and remembers our sins. Like the stains on the carpet that cannot be removed, our past is marked with the stain of sin. As an old proverb puts it, 'Old sins cast long shadows.' And there is an accounting day ahead.

We cannot remove sin from our life. Sin has corrupted every part of our being, our mind, our will and our affections. The corruption is inside us: 'Nothing outside a man can make him "unclean" by going into him. Rather, it is what comes out of a man that makes him "unclean"' (Mark 7:15). The situation is well summarized by Paul: 'I do not understand what I do. For what I want to do I do not do, but what I hate I do. I know that nothing good lives in me, that is, in my sinful nature. For I have the desire to do what is good, but I cannot carry it out. For what I do is not the good I want to do; no, the evil I do not want to do - this I keep on doing' (Romans 7:15, 18, 19).

God's character and nature are revealed and expressed in His law, and most of all in the Ten Commandments. As our Creator He has every right to require our obedience. But we cannot keep His law perfectly, no matter how hard we try. We may even choose to disobey it. Even when we try to keep God's laws we never achieve ten out of ten. There is no more power in us to follow His law than there is in a stone to go upwards of its own accord. The law requires what we are by nature quite unable to do. It requires perfect love in our hearts as well as actions which show our love. God's law identifies sin and makes us aware of our guilt. When our lives are put up against the plumb-line of God's law we see how crooked and imperfect we are. We are so much in debt to God's law that it may be said to be against us. The wonderful truth is that God has a special benefit in giving us His law. I don't go to a doctor unless in some way I know I am unwell; God's law directs me to Jesus Christ, through whom alone I can obtain God's forgiveness.

As our Creator He has every right to require our obedience. But we cannot keep His law perfectly

We cannot make amends by pleasing God, for God alone declares what pleases Him – it is not left to us to choose for Him. And God tells us that because we are sinful we cannot please Him. 'The sinful mind is hostile to God. It does not submit to God's law, nor can it do so. Those controlled by the sinful nature cannot please God' (Romans 8:7-8). Good works will not do (Ephesians 2:9).

We cannot even help the next generation. 'Folly is bound up in the heart of a child' (Proverbs 22:15). There was a cartoon in Punch magazine in which a mother says to an older child about her little brother: 'Go and find Johnny, see what he is doing and tell him not to.' Our children are no better than ourselves. Rather than help the next generation morally and spiritually, we seem at times to make things even more difficult for them (e.g. Genesis 6:5). We can see for ourselves how true this is today.

We are powerless to stop the approach of death. It has the key to all our homes. Sin leads to death, which is its wages (Romans 6:23). Death constantly shows us how helpless we are; it is no respecter of persons; we have no power over it; we cannot provide a substitute. 'No man has power over the wind to contain it; so no-one has power over the day of his death' (Ecclesiastes 8:8); the body returns to dust, and the spirit returns to God (Ecclesiastes 12:7). Death is the one certainty in our lives (Ecclesiastes 9:5).

We have no prospect of offering any satisfactory excuse when the Day of Judgment comes. Judgment is the certainty which follows men and women after death (Hebrews 9:27). Having no excuse for our sin, we will be in no better position then. Every one of us will stand hushed and guilty before Almighty God.

Unfortunately, even if we could change some of these things we would not do so because we are obstinately proud at heart. Human pride does not like the picture we have painted. If we dispute the fact that we are sinful, either we are lying or God is – and there is no doubt as to the right answer. 'If we claim to be without sin, we deceive ourselves and the truth is not in us' (1 John 1:8); 'If we claim we have not sinned, we make him out to be a liar and his word has no place in our lives' (1 John 1:10).

Our plight presents a pretty miserable picture when seen from God's viewpoint. But we should not run away from the truth. The situation leaves only one conclusion: God is the only one who can put our position right. And everything God does will be quite apart from what we deserve. Our very hopelessness as sinners shows us where our only real hope lies – with God alone.

God requires us to recognize that we cannot help ourselves before He helps us. Not surprisingly, the people who appreciated the

Lord Jesus Christ most when He went about were the obvious sinners. Those who thought they were all right missed God's forgiveness. On the other hand, those who admitted that they were sinners – like the tax-collector in Jesus' parable, who cried, 'God be merciful to me a sinner' – found complete forgiveness.

5 The Rescuer

'Mine disaster. Men trapped. Rescue operation in progress.' Words such as these have all too often hit the headlines. Rather like the case of men trapped in a mine, our only hope of deliverance from sin and the penalty it brings is if someone from outside intervenes to help – someone who is not himself trapped.

The qualifications for such a Rescuer can be listed because in different ways the Bible indicates them. He must share our humanity, so that He could enter into the feelings of those He was to rescue. He must be without any sin or blame himself, or else he would himself need help. He must be entirely satisfactory to God. He must have such merit in the eyes of God that, while God remains perfectly just because human sin is punished, yet He can reverse the sentence of condemnation which has been passed on men and women because He, the Rescuer, has been condemned in their place. The Rescuer must, therefore, be able to act in perfect accordance with God's wishes. No act of obedience must be beyond His reach.

Only God

God alone could provide a Rescuer – and that Rescuer was His own Son. 'For God so loved the world that he gave his one and only Son, that whoever believes in him shall not perish but have eternal life' (John 3:16). Before the world began God determined that His Son should be the Rescuer (1 Peter 1:20). It was not an emergency or last-minute arrangement. God

8 | Forgiveness

Forgiveness of sins is the first promise of the gospel. When Peter preached the first Christian sermon, on the Day of Pentecost, he concluded with the words, 'Repent and be baptised, every one of you, in the name of Jesus Christ for the forgiveness of your sins. And you will receive the gift of the Holy Spirit' (Acts 2:38). Some of Peter's hearers recognised their guilt in nailing the Son of God to a cross. Such sin and guilt must bring punishment. Nevertheless, they were offered complete exemption from the punishment they deserved.

Sin and guilt, as we have seen, constitute solid facts. Facts need to be faced, unpleasant as they may be. The Christian message is both 'good news' and 'the way to life' because it declares that there can be forgiveness - complete removal and cancellation of the guilt of our sin and its punishment.

A covenant

Centuries before the time of Jesus, through Old Testament prophets like Jeremiah, God promised a new covenant in which He would be able to say, 'I will forgive their wickedness and will remember their sins no more' (Jeremiah 31:34).

A covenant is a relationship between two people. When two people enter into a covenant, they enter into a special kind of relationship with each other, a relationship of a fixed and certain duration and nature. On account of Jesus Christ's death for sinners, a new and certain relationship with God is possible for us sinners. We can be completely forgiven and brought into God's family.

Forgiveness is the wiping out of the debt of sin. It is the cancellation of its guilt. It is the loosing of sinners from that which binds them. When we are forgiven by God, we feel and know a tremendous sense of release. In a moment, an intolerable burden has been lifted.

God's forgiveness is entirely undeserved on our part. It cannot be earned. Furthermore, it cannot be half-earned. A boy may want a bicycle, and his father may promise, 'You save half, and I'll give you half towards it.' But God's forgiveness is not at all like that: it is received as an undeserved gift, which is precisely what it is (Ephesians 2:8-9).

An assortment of men and women received God's forgiveness through Jesus while He was on earth. They each knew, without the slightest doubt, that they did not deserve forgiveness: for example, the woman who had been caught in adultery (John 8:1-11); the woman who was a notorious sinner (Luke 7:36-50); Zacchaeus, the cheat and swindler (Luke 19:1-10); the unscrupulous tax-collector (Luke 18:9-14); and the repentant thief (Luke 23:40-3).

Grudging forgiveness is human, not divine. God's forgiveness is rich - full and generous. The sacrifice of Jesus Christ was adequate for the sins of all who would believe - even the worst of sinners. God freely forgives, and He goes to great trouble to convince us of the fact. 'As far as the east is from the west, so far has he removed our transgressions from us' (Psalm 103:12). 'You have put all my sins behind your back' (Isaiah 38:17). 'You will tread our sins underfoot and hurl all our iniquities into the depths of the sea' (Micah 7:19). When God forgives, not a single sin is left unforgiven.

The simplest and most complete operation is the pressing of the delete button on a calculator. Whatever the sum - large or small - it is not only deleted but it is irretrievable. Through the blood of Jesus Christ, God can cancel the guilt of the sin in our heart. The conscience is made still and quiet. Access to God is open: no sin stands between to bar the way. Of course, once reconciled, we do not cease sinning. But as we confess our sins, God is faithful and just to forgive our sins and to cleanse us from all unrighteousness (1 John 1:9).

9 Right with God

Heaven and hell begin with either a good or a bad conscience. No peace compares with the peace of a good conscience. A wrong relationship with God coincides with a bad conscience towards Him, whereas a right relationship with God means a good and clear conscience.

Declared righteous

A right relationship with God can come about only as a man or woman is justified by faith (Romans 5:1). To 'justify' means to 'declare righteous' – in other words, made right with God so that we are at complete peace with him. The picture is of a man or woman on trial. The judge examines all the evidence and declares that they are not liable to any penalty, but entitled to all the privileges due to those who have kept the law. It is a miracle of God's kindness – or grace – to us through the death of His Son in our place.

Justification is the opposite of a sentence of condemnation. It deals with legal status and cancellation of legal liability. Everything about us as human beings makes such a declaration most desirable. By nature we are sinners. God's law condemns us. Its penalty hangs over our heads. But the good news of Jesus Christ means that God has provided a way by which we can be justified – a way by which He can justly declare that we are no longer liable to the penalty of death, but entitled to all the privileges of those who have kept the law.

'But how can this be?' we may well ask. God's law must be fulfilled.

We deserve to pay the penalty for disobedience if we fail to obey. The good news, however, is that God's demands have been met by the Lord Jesus Christ, acting on the behalf of sinners. He met all God's demands for obedience to the law; and He also died the death deserved by the disobedient. He bore the penalty of death which the law rightly pronounces on the guilty.

On the grounds of Jesus Christ's work for sinners, God is able justly to pronounce as 'righteous' all who trust in Jesus, because they are united to Jesus who fulfilled all the law for them, and bore their sin upon the cross. He took their sin, and now, as a result, His righteousness is reckoned to them (2 Corinthians 5:21). Justified, sinners are given a new status and a wonderful relationship with God. We are as much at peace with God as the Lord Jesus Christ is!

In the nineteenth century, Andrew Bonar, a Scottish minister, wrote in his diary, 'If there is one thing for which I bless the Lord more than another, it is this, that He has so far opened my eyes to see that Christ pleases the Father to the full, and that this is my ground of acceptance.'

Benefits of the relationship

Peace

Peace with God stands out as the first benefit of the new relationship with God (Romans 5:1). Previously we were rebels against Him. Our sins were a glaring offence against His law, and exposed us to God's enmity and wrath. But now we have peace with God through the death of the Lord Jesus Christ. Our guilty past may be cancelled. We can no longer be exposed to God's enmity and wrath.

The peace a child enjoys when with its parent is the peace the Christian enjoys with God. Jesus promised, 'In me you shall have peace.' (John 6:33). The peace carries with it free access to God (Romans 5:2). Not only is there forgiveness in the sense that punishment is remitted - as we have already seen - but a place of high favour with God is given. Access expresses the privilege of approaching or being introduced into the presence of someone of high position, especially a royal or divine person. The Lord Jesus Christ Himself ushers believers into their new state of favour and acceptance before God.

Joy

Not surprisingly, joy stands out as the second benefit of a right relationship with God (Romans 5:2). A sudden change of status has taken place. We have become a Christian, an heir of God and a joint-heir with Christ. We may look forward to an inheritance which lasts for ever. 'In my Father's house are many rooms; if it were not so, I would have told you. I am going there to prepare a place for you,' Jesus promised (John 14:2).

The joy that arises from the new relationship is so secure that trials and troubles cannot remove it (Romans 5:3). Indeed, difficulties or tribulations are a sign that God counts those who endure them as worthy of his kingdom (Acts 14:22; 2 Thessalonians 1:5). Suffering brings present and eternal benefits to the soul. Furthermore, God uses difficulties to cultivate endurance and steadfastness of character (Romans 5:3-5). Unpleasant circumstances make Christians recognise the true source of their joy - God Himself.

> **The joy that arises from the new relationship is so secure that trials and troubles cannot remove it...**

No joy is comparable to our joy in God when we possess a right relationship with Him (Romans 5:11). He becomes our joy and delight (Psalm 43:4), and He does not change. God wants His children to rise above merely thinking of their own happiness, even though that consists in knowing that they possess the glory of heaven. He wants their minds to be occupied with the contemplation of Him and their doing His will.

Christians have the prospect before them of knowing more and more of God Himself. Relationships deepen with time and experience. Whatever Christian believers need, God has for them. And the Lord Himself is their possession for ever. God's presence constitutes the happiness of heaven. 'You have made known to me the path of life; you will fill me with joy in your presence, with eternal pleasures at your right hand' (Psalm 16:11).

'This way to life,' says the signpost to Christianity. The right relationship Christians have with God means that they are able to 'rejoice in the hope of the glory of God' (Romans 5:2). Their hope is not the uncertain hope of the world in which we live, but a hope that cannot disappoint (Romans 5:5). The whole of eternity will reveal the splendours of possessing a right relationship with the one true God who sent His Son into the world to save sinners.

10 A new life

'How shall I keep it up if I become a Christian?' is a question we may naturally ask. Being a Christian leads to new standards of conduct and behaviour. This is a frightening prospect if we are required to maintain higher standards with our own ability. Even the old standards were beyond our power to fulfil. If this were the demand, the Christian life would be like failing one exam, only to be told immediately that a stiffer one lies ahead.

The power to live a new life is given to all who believe. 'You will receive the gift of the Holy Spirit,' Peter promised (Acts 2:38) and he assured his hearers that the promise was for all who followed them in hearing the gospel - the way to life (Acts 2:39).

'I will pour water on the thirsty land, and streams on the dry ground; I will pour out my Spirit on your offspring, and my blessing on your descendants,' God had promised (Isaiah 44:3). Jesus referred to such promises when He said, 'If anyone is thirsty, let him come to me and drink. Whoever believes in me, as the Scripture has said, streams of living water will flow from within him' (John 7:38). John comments, 'By this he meant the Spirit, whom those who believed in him were later to receive. Up to that time the Spirit had not been given, since Jesus had not yet been glorified' (John 7:39).

A Person

The power for living the Christian life, therefore, comes from a Person, not a thing. The Holy Spirit, the Third Person of the Trinity, is given to all who receive the gospel and put their trust in Jesus

Christ. When we say that God is a Trinity we are affirming that God is one in every way, in nature and being; but one in three distinct Persons – Father, Son and Holy Spirit. The word 'Trinity' is not found in the Bible but it sums up what the Bible teaches throughout concerning the mystery of God's Being. These three Persons are distinct and not simply different modes of appearance God uses in His relationship to us. Their true and equal divinity is insisted upon. It is a great mystery beyond my mind to understand, but a truth real to my experience. So, for example, I know that my prayers are to be addressed to God the Father; I pray in the name of Jesus because He is the way to the Father; and the Holy Spirit helps me to pray, as He aids me in many other things. Like any other person, He can be both pleased and offended. He is holy, and anything that is not holy grieves Him.

> **The power of the Spirit is not remote, but personal to each individual who believes.**

He executes God's purposes. The Father purposed the plan of salvation. The Son achieved the purpose of the plan by offering Himself upon the Cross. The Spirit executes the plan of salvation by applying to individual believers the benefits of what the Father purposed and the Son achieved.

The power of the Spirit is not remote, but personal to each individual who believes. The Holy Spirit lives within them; the Christian's body becomes His temple (1 Corinthians 3:16-17).

Benefits

The power of the Spirit means that the individual Christian is able to achieve what was impossible before. Imagine an old car making its way up a steep hill, hardly making the grade. With a look of pity you overtake quickly. Next week, you see it in front of you again. 'I'll overtake it,' you think to yourself. But as soon as you try, you find you cannot! A transformation in performance has taken place - the car has a new engine. It has power to lead a new life.

The Holy Spirit's presence in a person's life brings all kinds of benefits leading to beneficial activity. He brings an awareness of an intimate relationship with God. Prayer becomes a vital activity. Desires for pleasing God are prompted. He both creates a hunger for God's Word, and then proceeds to satisfy it. He makes the conscience sensitive to sin. He leads the Christian into service, equipping where necessary with special gifts and abilities. He brings aid in difficulties and power for holiness.

The tendency to live the old kind of life - the kind of life lived before becoming a Christian - remains with us. There is a battle, as might be expected, between the new life and the old - what the Bible calls 'the Spirit' and 'the sinful nature'. Unfortunately, Christians may fall into the snare of living according to their old life, and then temptation often defeats them. Victorious Christians live according to their new life, directed by the Holy Spirit.

'This way to life,' the Spirit continually says. Just as electricity flows when all is duly connected up, so God's promise is that as we 'live by the Spirit' we 'will not gratify the desires of the sinful nature' and the Spirit's fruit of Christ-likeness will grow in our lives (Galatians 5:16-26). Daily obedience brings a daily experience of God's peace: and this is life indeed.

11   Eternal life

The good news of Jesus Christ deals with our past in its offer of forgiveness. It enhances our present experience of life through a right relationship with God and the power to live a new life. It also holds promise for the future, through God's gift of eternal life and all that will mean.

The only real answer to death is life. There is no need for us to worry about death when we possess eternal life. Weird and fanciful ideas exist about life after death. Some suggest that heaven does not exist; others believe in reincarnation; yet others believe in heaven, but not hell. The Bible says that these ideas are false, and presents God's offer of eternal life, that is, sharing in the very life of God for ever. The explanation of the Cross, and of all that Jesus did, is that God did not desire that men and women should perish, but rather that they should have eternal life (John 3:16).

Thrilling prospect

Eternal life presents a wonderful prospect. Only God, of course, inhabits eternity. This fact gives some clue as to what eternal life is, for it is nothing other than the life lived by God Himself.

When we consider God as He is revealed in the Bible, we are presented with His holiness, His love, His power, and His eternity. Thus when we share in the life of God Himself, and have eternal life, we will experience the complete defeat of sin because *holiness* will characterise that life. No bitterness or hatred, or marred personal relationships will be present, for *perfect love* will mark all relationships. Failure and frustration will be absent for ever, for the *power of God* will be perfectly demonstrated in our lives. We will not be afraid of dying, for the *eternity of God* guarantees eternal and everlasting life to us.

All this may sound remote, seeming to refer to the future. But eternal life begins the moment we believe. The Lord Jesus Christ gives it to us now as a present possession. To become a Christian is to pass from death to life, to be spiritually alive to God, to have life turned from mere existence into real living.

The spiritual life which comes with the gift of the Holy Spirit is eternal life. Throughout our human life that spiritual life is nourished by fellowship with God, and a deepening knowledge of Him.

This benefit of the good news, like every other, is found in Jesus Christ alone. 'For as the Father has life in himself, so he has granted the Son to have life in himself' (John 5:26). Jesus merited life for sinners; through His death it was made possible. He paid 'the wages of sin' which is death (Romans 6:23), and eternal life may come to sinners, therefore, *through* Him (Romans 6:23). God the Father declared the way to life open for sinners by raising His Son from the dead. As Jesus Himself says, 'For my Father's will is that everyone who looks to the Son and believes in him shall have eternal life, and I will raise him up at the last day…I tell you the truth, he who believes has everlasting life' (John 6:40, 47).

12 | Repentance

The good news needs to be made personal: it does us no good in the abstract, or at a distance, or by report. Common sense tells us that good news requires a personal application. A remedy does no good until it is applied. While the medicine remains in the bottle, the body is not healed.

Jesus placed the emphasis on a sinner's personal response to Him. He said, 'I am the way and the truth and the life. No-one comes to the Father except through me…All that the Father gives me will come to me, and whoever comes to me I will never drive away' (John 14:6; 6:37). In the beginning of his gospel, John summarised the facts as follows: 'He came to that which was his own, but his own did not receive him. Yet to all who received him, to those who believed in his name, he gave the right to become children of God' (John 1:11-12).

The first step

The first step in making the good news of the Lord Jesus Christ personal is repentance. To avoid this first step is to disqualify ourselves straightaway. Jesus began His ministry with the words, 'The time has come…The kingdom of God is near. Repent and believe the good news!' (Mark 1:15).

Guilt made a convicted crowd ask Peter, 'What shall we do?' and his answer began with the word 'Repent!' (Acts 2:38). If we ask the same question today, the answer is still the same. God now 'commands all people everywhere to repent. For he has set a day when he will judge the world with justice by the man he has appointed. He has given proof of this to all men by raising him from the dead' (Acts 17:30).

What, then, is repentance? At its simplest, repentance is to turn from sin to God, as a result of a change of mind. It involves a new look at sin, and then a new look at ourselves. The experience cannot be pleasant. As a general rule, we tend to play down the unpleasant facts of life, particularly when they concern us personally. Sin is one such unpleasant and uncomfortable subject. When we are compelled to discuss it, we may make light of it, and speak perhaps of hereditary factors, extenuating circumstances, natural weaknesses, and so forth. In fact, we will sometimes talk about sin in every conceivable way, except as it really is: a horrible disease of the human heart, displeasing to God, and a great offence to His holiness.

Repentance involves a new look at sin because it means seeing how displeasing it is in God's sight. But the new look does not stop there; it moves on to a new look at ourselves - seeing ourselves as sinners in God's sight, so that the cry is wrung from us, 'Against you, you only, have I sinned' (Psalm 51:4).

Sinfulness is seen to lie not only in the fact that we have sinned here and there, but also that we are sinners by nature and in practice - and deserve only to be condemned. 'For troubles without number surround me; my sins have overtaken me, and I cannot see. They are more than the hairs of my head, and my heart fails within me (Psalm 40:12). 'More than the hairs of my head' – when we have recognised our sinfulness like this, we have begun to repent.

> **Repentance involves a new look at sin because it means seeing how displeasing it is in God's sight.**

But merely to recognise sin for what it is, and our personal sinfulness, is insufficient. Repentance also means a change of mind and heart about sin, resulting in a change of behaviour. More than sorrow for the past is required. Sorrow must be accompanied by a change of mind and attitude towards sin, together with a desire to live a new and better life. Property may have to be returned and apologies made. Such restitution is an evidence of genuine repentance. In the 1920s there was something of a revival in Northern Ireland through the preaching of a Presbyterian minister, W P Nicholson, when thousands were converted. It was said that Harland and Wolff, the great ship-builders, had to open a special building for the return of stolen tools.

A fundamental break with the past and a determination to please God indicate genuine repentance. But repentance will have only just begun, for it is a continuing activity. Once the break with sin has been made, the new attitude to sin must be renewed every day as new temptations present fresh opportunities of showing our desire to please the living and true God. God gives us His Spirit to help us to do this each day.

When we have the Cross of the Lord Jesus Christ clearly in view, and realise the almost unimaginable kindness and love of God towards us, to repent stands out as the least we can do, in view of what our sin did to God's Son.

13 | Believing

The first step is repentance; the second is belief or faith. The most important thing about belief is the One in whom we are to believe. To enter into the 'good' of the good news, to find 'the way to life', we are commanded to believe on the Lord Jesus Christ.

The facts

Certain facts have to be understood first concerning Jesus of Nazareth. First, He is *the Christ*. When our first parents, Adam and Eve, rebelled against God, He promised a Deliverer, the Messiah. The Jews spoke of Him as God's Anointed One. That is what the word Messiah means. Translated into Greek 'Messiah' became 'Christos' or 'Christ'. The Old Testament prophets spoke much of His character and His work. The manner of His birth was described, and His ministry and death were prophesied in great detail (Isaiah 53). Everything in the life of Jesus took place precisely as the prophets had promised, and, in particular, the central events of His life - His Death and Resurrection (1 Corinthians 15:3-4).

Secondly, He is *the Lord*. The title 'Lord' does not have much meaning today, but it was charged with meaning in the first century when it was used for Jesus. The same Greek word was used for translating the Old Testament word for God, and it was also used of the Roman emperors when they were worshipped as gods. Jesus Christ is God. His human conception in the womb of the virgin Mary was miraculous - the work of the Holy Spirit. His miracles displayed a power which could have come only from God. The conviction that He was God grew upon His intimate disciples and became essential to all that they knew to be true of Him. Positive proof that He is God was given in the Resurrection.

Thirdly, He is *the Saviour*. His name Jesus means 'God is my Saviour'. As the Old Testament had promised, sin was the problem He had to come to deal with it. He died to bear away sin.

Belief

The way to life is to believe in Jesus: to believe that He is the Saviour, the Christ, and the Lord. But just believing these facts in the mind, of course, is not enough. Merely to say we believe these facts without any action sets us on the way to life as much as hugging a time-table takes us on a train journey.

For ourselves, individually, we have to say from our heart, 'You are the Christ, the Son of the living God' (Matthew 16:16).

Together with this personal belief that Christ is the Son of God goes the personal belief that Christ died for our sins. 'The Son of God...loved me and gave himself for me' (Galatians 2:20). 'Christ Jesus came into the world to save sinners - of whom I am the worst' (1 Timothy 1:15).

And so faith, or belief, moves beyond the facts to trusting a Person. 'Yet to all who received him, to those who believed in his name, he gave the right to become children of God' (John 1:12). 'For God so loved the world that he gave his one and only Son, that whoever believes in him shall not perish but have eternal life' (John 3:16).

The stand which is taken upon these facts, bringing confidence in the Person of the Lord Jesus Christ, involves the abandonment of all confidence in human merit and works, for the obtaining of salvation. No confidence in outward things, such as race, social status, respectability or good deeds (Titus 3:5) can bring forgiveness or salvation.

The place of the Bible

Belief in the Lord Jesus Christ is the way to life. The instrument God uses to bring us to faith is the Bible, or 'the Word of God', as it is called. 'Faith comes from hearing the message, and the message is heard through the word of Christ' (Romans 10:17). The Bible writers were inspired by the Holy Spirit, who was thus, in a sense, the supreme Author. His purpose is to present the Lord Jesus Christ to us, and the Bible is simply full of Jesus. As the facts concerning Him are presented to us by the Bible, the Holy Spirit convinces us as individuals of their truth - He is the Spirit of truth (John 16:13). As a consequence, God's message is received, not as the word of men, but as what it truly is, the actual Word of God (1 Thessalonians 2:13).

As the truth of the Christian faith is recognised, the Holy Spirit applies the truth to us as individuals. He uses God's law to reveal our personal sin and accountability before God (Galatians 3:21-24; Romans 7:7). And by this means He brings conviction of sin leading to repentance (John 16:8-11; Acts 2:27, 38), which, as we have seen, is the first step in making the good news personal. Having convinced us of sin, the Holy Spirit makes plain the remedy for sin - the sinner's Saviour. The good news of Jesus and the benefits of His Death and Resurrection come home to our mind and heart with strong conviction.

Those who possess such faith may be encouraged, for it is God's gift to them, and God does not take it back

And so faith comes about, not through the force of any subtle argument but through the power of the Holy Spirit (1 Corinthians 2:4). Those who possess such faith may be encouraged, for it is God's gift to them, and God does not take it back, having given it (Philippians 1:6). Those without faith may likewise be encouraged, for if they will deliberately put themselves into situations and places where God's Word is faithfully preached, and if they will read it for themselves seeking the Lord Jesus Christ through it, they will find Him for themselves, and in finding Him they will have found living faith in God, and the way to life.

14 | Declaring your faith

When people have been in a perilous position - say, for example, in a pit disaster or an air or sea accident - and have escaped, there will be those eagerly awaiting them. They will want to hear their story as to what happened and their testimony as to how they escaped. And those rescued will be prepared to speak, most of all, on behalf and in praise of their rescuer or rescuers. Probably for the rest of their life they will return to the subject, and tell every new acquaintance about it.

The most perilous position in the world is to be an unforgiven sinner. To be such is to have our feet on a road which leads to certain death, condemnation, judgment and hell. When we are rescued from that predicament, we have something to talk about. Most of all we want to testify concerning our Rescuer - the Lord Jesus Christ.

Repentance and faith - in a sense - are not sufficient. Public or open confession of Jesus Christ is the final step which makes the others complete. Now, of course, the mere saying of so many words publicly does not make a person a Christian. Jesus said, 'Not everyone who says to me, "Lord, Lord," will enter the kingdom of heaven' (Matthew 7:21). But having said that, we may as well think of a shaft of light hiding in the darkness as think of a person having faith and keeping it secret.

The Bible is clear: 'If you confess with your mouth, "Jesus is Lord," and believe in your heart that God raised him from the dead, you will be saved. For it is with your heart that you believe and are justified, and it is with your mouth that you confess and are saved' (Romans 10:9, 10).

We are commanded to declare with our lips what we have come to believe in our hearts, namely, that Jesus, the Saviour, is the Lord. We declare Him to be the only Saviour (Acts 4:12). It is true that nothing is added to the Lord Jesus Christ by these declarations. But the world at large remains ignorant of who He really is, and this ignorance is dispelled only as Christians, by their declarations, make it plain.

God requires that those who find 'the way to life' should confess unashamedly before the world His Son as Lord and Saviour (Matthew 10:32). Baptism, the Lord's Supper and membership of the local church all have their place in the individual's confession of Jesus in the community in which he or she lives.

There is no by-passing the confession of faith in the Lord Christ if we would enter the way of life. He commands it (Matthew 10:32); God the Father requires it (Philippians 2:11); and the Holy Spirit prompts every genuine declaration of Jesus as Lord (1 Corinthians 12:3). Furthermore, those who have found 'the way to life' in Jesus Christ know only too well that they owe such a declaration to Him, for confessing Him before others is the most direct means of honouring Him, and of bringing others to acknowledge Him. Like a believer long ago, we find ourselves compelled to say, 'He put a new song in my mouth, a hymn of praise to our God' (Psalm 40:3). 'Faith by itself, if it is not accompanied by action, is dead' (James 2:17). The first work of true faith is open confession of Jesus Christ. A sound bulb, properly planted, brings forth a healthy flower. Sound faith planted in the heart brings forth the glad declaration of Jesus Christ by life and lip.

To resist this truth is to disobey the Lord Jesus Christ, displease God the Father and grieve the Holy Spirit. What is more, it brings the individual within the compass of the warning Jesus gave, 'If anyone is ashamed of me and my words in this adulterous and sinful generation, the Son of Man will be ashamed of him when he comes in his Father's glory with the holy angels' (Mark 8:38).

15 | You have only begun

Becoming a Christian is no more the end of the Christian life than being born into the world is the end of a human life - it is only the beginning. The way in which a person becomes a Christian is clearly explained in the Bible: first, there must be repentance before God for sin; secondly, there must be faith in the Lord Jesus Christ as our personal Saviour; and, thirdly, there must be the public declaration of our faith in the Lord Jesus Christ. But these are only the beginnings.

Continuing to repent

Repentance is not a once-for-all act. When repentance is first professed, we tend to think that we recognise all our sins, and that we turn from them all. But this is not the case. While we are sincere enough, we only partly repent at first. When we repent, we tend to do so more because of sin's troublesomeness than because of its sinfulness. We do not easily see how we may have been deceiving ourselves about sin for years.

The older Christians grow, the more they realise how sinful they are; this means that the Christian life is necessarily one of continuing repentance. An example of this is the apostle Paul. Early in his Christian life he called himself 'the least of the apostles' (1 Corinthians 15:9). In middle life he called himself 'the least of all God's people' (Ephesians 3:8). At the close of his life he called himself 'the worst' of sinners (1 Timothy 1:15). That was not Paul going backwards in his knowledge of God, but forwards. Every day we are to turn from sin afresh, so that we may serve the Lord with all our heart.

Living by faith

Faith also is a continuous principle. The first exercise of faith is putting our trust personally in the Lord Jesus Christ as the Holy Spirit presents Him to us in the Bible. But that is only the beginning. Faith, to begin with, is but a small thing; it needs to grow. At first, faith may be thought of as a feeling or a succession of feelings, instead of an influential principle. Now we must grow in the exercise of faith. The larger our understanding of the Person and Work of our Lord Jesus Christ, the more we exercise faith in Him. As there is no end to discovering more about the wonder of our Saviour's Person and Work, so there is no end to growing in the exercise of faith. The Christian life is lived by faith; by means of it we discover the reality of the Lord Jesus' unseen help. Living by faith is to have our whole activity and character, inward and outward, permanently influenced and directed by our faith in God through His Son.

Witnessing

Declaring and confessing the Lord Jesus Christ before others is a daily task, and to use our lives and lips to speak of Him to others is the work and privilege of a lifetime. God has been so good to us in Jesus Christ that we cannot help saying, 'Give thanks to the Lord, for he is good; his love endures for ever. Let the redeemed of the Lord say this - those he redeemed from the hand of the foe' (Psalm 107:1-2).

...to use our lives and lips to speak of Him to others is the work and privilege of a lifetime.

The words of Jesus to someone He healed are relevant to all who find salvation in Him: 'Go home to your family and tell them how much the Lord has done for you and how he has had mercy on you' (Mark 5:19). We are not to be afraid or troubled by what people may say about us. Rather, as Peter urges, 'Always be prepared to give an answer to everyone who asks you to give the reason for the hope that you have. But do this with gentleness and respect' (1 Peter 3:15). Such a task will not be difficult if, like Paul, we can say,

'I am not ashamed of the gospel, because it is the power of God for the salvation of everyone who believes' (Romans 1:16).

Joining a local church

All start on 'the way to life' as spiritual babies. For healthy development a baby requires the security of a family. For the spiritual well-being, protection and security of His spiritual children, God provides the fellowship of the local church. And our first concern, therefore, as new Christians should be to find the local church where we will receive the most spiritual help and encouragement. Having found it, we should identify ourselves with it by membership. The early Christians 'devoted themselves to the apostles' teaching and to the fellowship, to the breaking of bread and to prayer' (Acts 2:42), and they set an example for all who join 'the way to life' to follow. Belonging to God's family, the meetings of the family are not to be neglected (Hebrews 10:25). A sign of spiritual health is the feeling expressed in the words, 'I rejoiced with those who said to me, "Let us go to the house of the Lord"' (Psalm 122:1).

As we involve ourselves in the life of the local church, we will discover opportunities for serving God in fellowship with others. Just as the individual parts of our body have differing functions, so Christians have different, yet complementary, functions as members of the body of Christ, the Church. Never hesitate to offer your help, and pray that God will lead you and those who guide you concerning the service you should offer.

Praying to God

As babies must soon learn to talk, so spiritual infants should learn to pray. Trust in the Lord is expressed by pouring out our hearts before Him (Psalm 62:8). The Lord Jesus says to the new Christian, 'Until now you have not asked for anything in my name. Ask and you will receive, and your joy will be complete' (John 16:24). As we seek to obey the Lord Jesus Christ, we may have confidence that if we ask anything according to God's will He will hear us and grant what we ask (1 John 5:14-15). Learn to pray about everything

(Philippians 4:6-7); have at least one set time every day when you give time to prayer; and turn to God throughout the day as often as you feel the need and have the opportunity.

Reading the Bible

Children learn to read as well as to talk. Spiritual infants learn to read the Bible in a way that was not possible before. 'All Scripture is God-breathed and is useful for teaching, rebuking, correcting and training in righteousness,' so that we 'may be thoroughly equipped for every good work' (2 Timothy 3:16-17). Give time to reading the Bible, remembering that every part is written for your instruction (Romans 15:4). 'Hide God's Word in your heart' (Psalm 119:11). Be as regular in reading your Bible as you are in eating food each day. Make a rule: no Bible, no breakfast!

Yes, you are only beginning! You need to be sure of the ABC of the Christian faith. The Bible provides all the information we require to make us sure of what God wants us to know and believe about Himself and His purposes. Subjects such as repentance, faith, the work of the Holy Spirit, the resurrection of the dead, and eternal judgment should be at our fingertips (Hebrews 6:1,2). The study of subjects like these from the Bible adds strength to our faith and provides food to our soul. There are wonderful truths to discover and appreciate, such as the hope to which God calls us, the wealth and glory of the share He offers us among His people in their eternal inheritance, and how vast are the resources of His power open to those who trust in Him (Ephesians 1:17-19).Beware, however, of mere head knowledge. Be determined, above all else, to grow in your real knowledge and experience of the Lord Jesus Christ. Study your Bible with that intention; wanting to know more of it that you may know more of Him. Call upon God's Spirit to help you in this. Such a call never goes unanswered.

Knowing God's forgiveness

You must know what to do when you sin. Being a Christian does not mean being sinless. While sin's power is broken in our lives as Christians, sadly we still sin, and we will continue to do so until we leave this life and lose our sinful nature.

God does not want us to pretend that we have not sinned when in fact we know that we have. Even as young children run to their parents when they fall over, run to God in prayer when you sin, seeking His immediate forgiveness. 'If we confess our sins, he is faithful and just and will forgive us our sins and purify us from all unrighteousness' (1 John 1:9). He promises such forgiveness to us for the sake of the Lord Jesus Christ. Sin can never remove your relationship with God through the Lord Jesus, but it can spoil your experience of it if you fail to confess your sins and receive the blessing of God's renewed forgiveness.

Discovering God's will

God has a will for your life, both generally and specifically. His declared will is that you should be holy; this means that you should abstain from immorality of any sort. Learn to gain mastery over your body, to respect and honour it, not giving way to lust as may have been the case in the past (1 Thessalonians 4:2-5).Strive to be like the Lord Jesus Christ, and aim at what you know pleases God. The Holy Spirit's presence in your life makes achievable what would otherwise be an impossible task.

And then for every part of your life - including your career, your relationships, and your service in the church - God has perfect purposes and plans. 'Trust in the Lord with all your heart and lean not on your own understanding; in all your ways acknowledge him, and he will make your paths straight' (Proverbs 3:5-6). Again, the Holy Spirit is always at hand to help you. He will use the Bible as a lamp to your feet and a light to your path (Psalm 119:105), helping

Much of what we have said may be summed up in the one word that is the secret of success in the Christian life - obedience.

you to understand and discover God's will. All God's purposes for you are good, perfect and acceptable (Romans 12:2), and you may rest in that confidence when you do not understand what

God may be doing in your life.

You have only just begun! But do not be bewildered. Much of what we have said may be summed up in the one word that is the secret of success in the Christian life - obedience. Obeying God's truth - the Bible - is the secret of success. Joshua's secret may be ours: 'Do not let this Book of the Law depart from your mouth; meditate on it day and night, so that you may be careful to do everything written in it. Then you will be prosperous and successful' (Joshua 1:8).

But let your confidence be in the fact that while, from one point of view, you have only just begun, it is, in fact, God Himself who has begun the good work in you. 'He who began a good work in you will carry it on to completion until the day of Christ Jesus' (Philippians 1:6). When God begins a work, He completes it. 'The one who calls you is faithful and he will do it'(1 Thessalonians 5:24). Mark records a story that illustrates how certain it is that God will complete His work in our lives. Some people brought a blind man to Jesus, and begged Him to touch him. 'He took the blind man by the hand and led him outside the village. When he had spat on the man's eyes and put his hands on him, Jesus asked, "Do you see anything?" he looked up and said, "I see people; they look like trees walking around." Once more Jesus put his hands on the man's eyes. Then his eyes were opened, his sight was restored, and he saw everything clearly' (Mark 8:23-25).

Starting out on 'the way to life', you may at first feel that you are rather like the blind man Jesus healed. You are beginning to see, but your vision is blurred and not as clear as you would like. Do not be discouraged. Continue to obey the Lord Jesus Christ every day, guided by the Bible's teaching. Soon you will see more clearly; and the more you live in obedience to the Lord Jesus, the more wonderful you will find the Christian life to be. And all that we discover now is the merest foretaste of what is ahead of us when we go to be where the Lord Jesus Christ is. He is the way - and the truth and the life - and He prepares a place for us in His heavenly kingdom. He is our way to life!